My Late Heart

Jose Lopez

BookLeaf Publishing

India | USA | UK

Presentation by *BookLeaf Publishing*

Web: www.bookleafpub.com

E-mail: info@bookleafpub.com

ISBN: 9789360945657

First edition 2024

Grace Vazquez

PREFACE

This is my first and perhaps only printed work.

The Strap

Don't you think I've been strapped to you this
whole time
Not since we met, not since apology, and not
since regret
Just look when we lied, it burned to fray a house
But tight without burn the strap still defined.

Didn't it wrap again when
Tied and tense we told our lips to meet,
while you hung upside down the ground
and the tree felt my weight up right
Tight and no burn and didn't snap when you
drew to my lips
Who let these kids kiss.

But then, said the time
The strap was worn, tearing red
An end acted dumb, and let slip his mind
Tight, unburned, not snapped but then stretched,
the end still belongs to the strap of my bliss.

I'm Blind

I hurt, I cried, I regretted and fled
With a trail of tears behind me, flooding basic
sight
I follow thee blindly, love of my life.

Handful

My hands are still getting past the habit of
having you in them
And I promise, its not to find bliss in
Each of my fingers directly needs to be told to
stop missing you
But of course they only ask
And they turn to not listen
My thumb starts
I cannot feel, what has been misled?
My middle, index, ring
where are the bends, they're no longer sitting.
My pinky's right is honest and feels no
difference
But the left side will be blue until it's found back
its mission.

Without Her

It strikes me, the image of this girl
Her head is lamp lit, feeding seas of that
muzzled brown hair to me. She turns and tides
wash both the bronze jewel eyes.
The word ache is overused in my opinion, so
how am I to describe my level of distress during
this flood of without-her. I see she's, maybe
drowning, and calling my name. Call it, call it,
need me. I know I'll reach her hand soon.
Although each day reminds my heart of another
crawl through cold storm, and gray has fallen to
my eyes,
it's right then that source to keep me fed rescues.
And with she I can stand.

Honey

My hair is cold honey
Don't you be long
It's been too late for my habit, it grew real fond
Give me your hands to my head, please
and nothing instead.

Addressing Color

Today all of my beaches are dressed in green
And the sand grains bask at the yellow yell.
Hello I am the sun she says, what more could
she tell.

Heavy and Rust

It's weird, I only feel jealousy.
Really it's all the weight I hold
There's no fear or worry on the welds of my
trust.
I swear it's only jealousy, uncut and pure.
There's nothing to do but feel it, heavy, and rust.

Doll

I'm a boy with my doll
I hope she plays nice
I think she knows my eyes are glass-fragile too
right
My arms at her will, something feels off
Its usually me leading toys to the ball
But sit down and stay and I'm feeling all small
She's right about loving me, just like a doll.

My Day Isn't Here

Hardly seconds of sunlight brush past the cold
and soft cloud canvas
Addressing the spark of long stars streaking at
blue beside my feet
I'm upset with dry feet while they're all dancing
in the gleams
What it seems, while they jump and blue waves
bounce, is that my day is not here with me.
And so my mind races in ask, where to and
where is she
The woman in red pointed to the nice act that
made her happy, and again the water screamed
Bright flashing white coins flipping through sea
But what she showed was the sun and not close
to relief
At least my mind is clear, my day will obsess
until you're next to me

Pobrecito

Que pobrecito mi bonito, escucha lo que llanta
sin ti
Mi sangre me duele, y siente que se sale
porque quedo muy lejos de sonreír
Que pobrecito mi bonito, no ves que ya no
quiere sufrir
No tiene ni ojos, y sin tu guía no hay fin.
Que pobrecito mi bonito, ya anda más rojo que
nunca y
De seguro le falta aire, pero me ha dicho que
será suficiente el saber llegar de ti.
Muy muy pobre, mi bonito bien estar.

Beauty Don't Stay

I grieved while I walked out to day
Light warmth on my skin and no haze.
Shadows were bright on clouds rolling white
And blue made its sentence today.
Birds spoke in words, trees have felt worse
But that green pushed my limit past bay.
See without you is to be so sick yet breathing
And the grass feels my self needs a save
But today I woke up, needing my grieving
So leave me blind, beauty don't stay.

Well Well Well

I understand well
The indignation that was felt by
cause now it's me who's crawling
at the bottom of, well, what's missing.
Practically shouting, why pretend you don't hear
me
Maybe your love fell too deep.
What's drowning those ears, there's none inside
mine
I thought it was me above this whole time.
Feel it, whatever drives your attention
and I'll feel the violent lack of pull just as well.

(You left me on read for an hour)

Look At Me, Please

Do I catch your eyes at the prettiest times,
how do they know to be right.
Serious blame on your gaze, for what my watch
doesn't tell me
Beauty is a place in time.
Now the watch ticks in fear.
Serving purpose less often.
Since, you, the culprit, it feels that his meaning
has bled.
Eyes can't say the time, but it's yours flooding
mine
that clocks turn unclear once again.
All the reason I find
to stamp names on a time
You bury beneath your simple bold sight.

Mexico One

Amber on my fingers. I closed my eyes,
so my fingertips turned red without me.
But I felt it, slowly, because our hesitant noses
led bluntly.
A couple of seconds before our lips connected,
we knew nothing would stop.
In between my hand and your skin, we met with
no boundary
And then that no separation bit softly.

Mexico Two

Eyes pull on your heart until you pick up the
camera. This subject is special. Your heart
doesn't stop.
Captured in perfect chemical
she'll be there forever
stamped by the same light as your eyes
How many lights will I have of you.
Who will we show them to
How we will look back at them
Through our own museum
We'll live again and again

Mexico Three

I come to you with my heart—it's full of bad
habit and it's already loved. I come with this
heart that hurts when I think about them, but this
heart that chose it just to think of you.

Mexico Four

Let me be blunt and say I don't think distance is going to work out well for us Grace. I think too much of you, you're distracting to the highest degree. I'm lucky these two weeks there's really no responsibilities to carry, I can think about you freely. Apart, we're both too busy. We graze a few words to each other each day but it's not enough. Not even the call at the airport was.

It's a shame Thursday was the only day we had like that, I want to be at the edge of your lips again. I want to make you laugh with selfish intent. I want to know how you feel about me, right in front of you. This is bad.

I can't wait until I come back. I want to be sick of you by the time you leave.

At Night

At night shadows don't exist
Dull dark grey bleeds off the walls into
everything else
If this is true why are you here.
Darker than no light
I feel you, coming from behind.

god damn aviator jacket

Ground dirt colored aviator
Creased where it's glowing, so refined
The leather boasts at the stitch lines,
Where function met it and bred fine

I'm wise, it says to fill the cold of my eyes
And practical, if you could hear what it said
In my head it's mine
Screaming coffee and tense knuckles
Because that made-up mirror denies

A match with my hair
A sync with my voice

But god damn, that aviator would be my choice

Blue

I love blue
Blue all over
Blue as my pack
Blue on my back

What color should I be, the sky may ask
Why I won't love you unless you're blue
Dark, dark and so blue.

Juan

My hero, I will suffer too much
My old man, I should not even think it
It was today that gray colored your face
And I've realized what it means to be blind
You worked too hard and turns out old
I never want to hold your rough hands in mine